Like priests worshiping before some ancient deity, the

Cadillac dealers gazed in rapt silence for a moment. Then,

perhaps triggered by a highlight caught in the Florentine curve

of the rear window, or perhaps it was out of some common

impulse of gratitude, suddenly, spontaneously, they broke into

an applause charged with genuine emotion. Here it was:

nineteen gorgeous feet, two-and-a-half solid tons of American

Dream—and all theirs!

What they were seeing, as well they knew, was not just a

car, but an institution.

—William H. Whyte, Jr., Fortune, 1955

AMERICA WORKED.

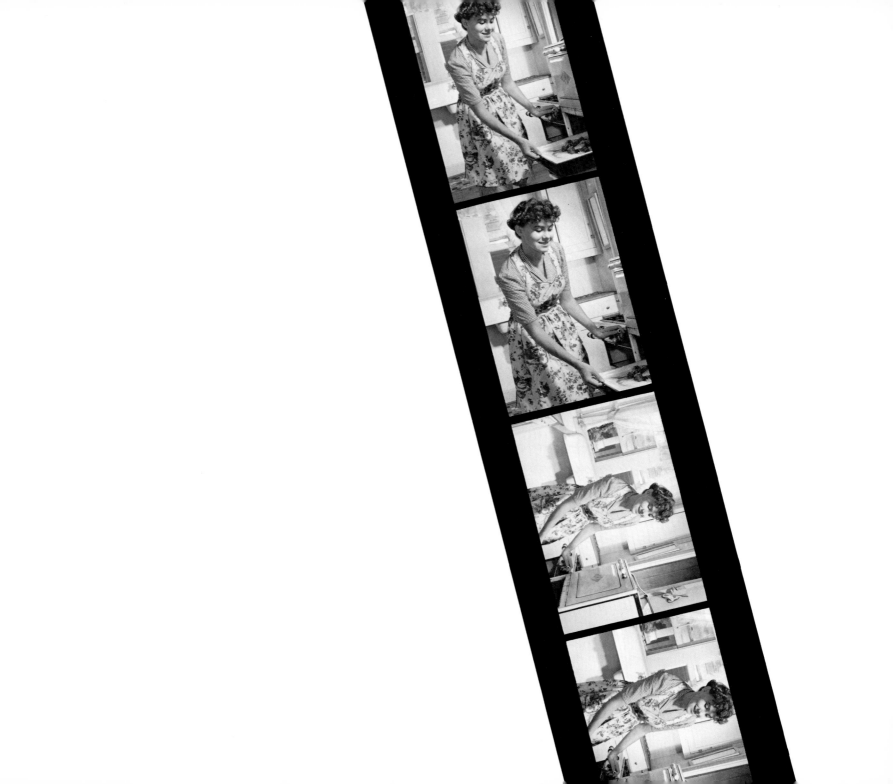

*H*ousewives consistently report that one of the most

pleasurable tasks of the home is making a cake. Psychologists

were put to work exploring this phenomenon for merchandising

clues. James Vicary made a study of cake symbolism and came

up with the conclusion that ''baking a cake is traditionally acting

out the birth of a child.''

—*Vance Packard,* The Hidden Persuaders, *1957*

THE 1950S PHOTOGRAPHS OF DAN WEINER

AMERICA WORKED.

BY WILLIAM A. EWING

WITH AN INTRODUCTION BY LIONEL TIGER

HARRY N. ABRAMS, INC., PUBLISHERS, NEW YORK

Project Director/Robert Morton
Editing and Design/William A. Ewing

Acknowledgments

First and foremost, I would like to thank Sandra Weiner for her active participation in this
project from its inception. She was immensely helpful in the search for key images and
had much of interest to say about Dan's own thoughts and working methods. The project
developed into a true collaboration.

I wish also to thank the anthropologist Lionel Tiger for contributing an amusing and
perceptive overview of the period; Robert Menschel, whose enthusiastic response to an
early layout of the book brought it to the attention of the Museum of Modern Art; and
John Szarkowski and Susan Kismaric, whose enthusiasm developed into a supportive
exhibition.

I also wish to thank Luis Barrios and David Spear for new prints from Dan's negatives;
in addition, David Spear helped with the preparation of the contact strip material.
Suzanne Barth also deserves thanks for lending Sandra Weiner a hand on a number of
occasions. At *Fortune*, Marshall Loeb gave the project his support while Michele McNally
graciously allowed me the run of the archives.

I owe special thanks to William H. Whyte Jr. for his permission to quote extensively
from his writings, and for his recollections of Dan Weiner at work. Lastly, I wish to thank
Max Kozloff, David Mellor, Henrietta Brackman, Heidi Hummler, Steve Dietz, and Ed Zern
for advice, information, and encouragement.
W. A. E.

Ewing, William A.
 America worked: the 1950s photographs of Dan Weiner/by William A. Ewing; with
 an introduction to the period by Lionel Tiger. p. cm.
Includes index.
ISBN 0-8109-1177-9
 1. United States—Social life and customs—1945–1970—Pictorial works.
 2. United States–Description and travel—1940–1960—Views.
I. Weiner, Dan, 1919–1959.   II. Title.   88-7474
E169.02.E95 1989
973.92—dc 19

Photographs copyright ©1989 Sandra Weiner
Introduction copyright ©1989 Lionel Tiger
Text copyright ©1989 William A. Ewing
Quotations from William H. Whyte, Jr., *The Organization Man* copyright © 1956, 1984 by
William H. Whyte, Jr., reprinted by permission of Simon & Schuster, Inc.
Published in 1989 by Harry N. Abrams, Incorporated, New York. All rights reserved. No
part of the contents of this book may be reproduced without the written permission of
publisher

A Times Mirror Company

Printed and bound in the United States of America.

CONTENTS

About the Photographer

William A. Ewing

Dan Weiner embarked on an illustrious career as a photojournalist in 1949. He died only ten years later, on assignment in Kentucky, when a small plane, piloted by the subject of his story, slammed into a mountainside during a freak snowstorm. The personal dimensions of the tragedy, the death of a beloved husband and an adored father, were compounded by a public loss: the many readers of *Fortune*, *Collier's*, the *New York Times*, and a number of other influential publications would no longer see through the eyes of an astute photographer. Just thirty-nine years old, he was at the peak of his powers. "The small rank of fine photographers has been cruelly thinned by the loss of Dan Weiner," wrote Edward Steichen. More bluntly, Arthur Miller added, "The death of such a phenomenon is inadmissible."

Over the decade of the fifties Weiner used the tools of his craft to depict a particular vision of American life—a *working* America, seen in supermarkets and shopping centers, offices and boardrooms, schools and hospitals, farms and factories. But in the photographs, while many of Weiner's Americans seem clearly enchanted with the fruits of their labors (the new suburbia, jet-age automobiles, and a dizzying array of novel goods and services), and display with unbridled pride the toys and badges of entrepreneurial success, others cling to faltering farms, or huddle in the corners of decrepit old-age homes, discarded by a prodigal society.

His rich portrayal of the nation during a period of explosive growth and economic expansion was thoughtfully constructed, at once respectful and caring, inquisitive and critical. Nowadays our main window on the fifties (or to use the appropriate idiom, *picture window*) is provided by the kitsch of advertising and promotional imagery, or what Marshall McLuhan called "expensive and influential programs of commercial education." As idealized, cosmeticized, and ultimately ridiculous as that picture was, the very ubiquity of the imagery ensured that much of it would survive: current books and magazine articles tend to rely too much on this inventory for anecdotes and surveys of the period, further perpetuating the deceptive gloss.

Dan Weiner, in a study by Sandra
Weiner, while the couple was
stationed in Georgia prior to
his career as a photojournalist.

Weiner's view was quite different: he was able to see behind the facade of the American dream and reveal its frayed edges and split seams. His work reminds us that not all Americans of that era constantly cruised in shark-finned convertibles (with the male always at the wheel), or relaxed on "Colonial" sofas in split-level "rec rooms" admiring their new Venetian blinds and wall-to-wall synthetic "miracle" carpets—even had they wanted to! And when they *did* manage to acquire affluent trappings, their expressions and hesitant gestures often suggest a certain unease, as if the wonderful things that had befallen them might as readily be snatched away. In light of the tremendous attention given today to the issue of decline—of American power and prestige, on the one hand, and society and culture, on the other—the tendency to perceive the fifties as a bright and golden era is understandable. Weiner's hard-nosed truthfulness comes as a welcome antidote to this giddy picture.

Many of the pictures in this book are published for the first time. Among those that were published, I have partially broken up the original "stories" in which they were laid out by the magazines and regrouped the material according to major themes of the period.

The chapter Prospects and Promises takes a look at the widespread belief in progress and a decade of rampant if naive optimism. A Woman's World is fascinating from a feminist perspective. Except for nurses, teachers, and other members of "feminine" professions, the women appear startlingly passive, a culturally engineered attitude at the time widely held to be a woman's nature. Other chapters take their titles from popular and influential books of the period: anyone who was an adult in those years will remember the enormous interest stirred by William H. Whyte, Jr.'s *The Organization Man*, David Riesman's *The Lonely Crowd*, and Vance Packard's *The Hidden Persuaders*.

Regrouping these photographs raises the question of the weight to be given their original context. In fact, the photographer himself was seldom happy with the way the magazines used his material. Weiner was fundamentally disenchanted with the world of magazine publishing—he often observed that a photographer was called in to "fix a hole, like a plumber," and that his pictures were used out of context. (Weiner was not always displeased with the periodicals' display of his work: *Fortune* and *Collier's* in particular employed his photographs most effectively on a number of occasions.) Large issues, such as the rise of black political activism, which he handled in his Montgomery, Alabama, pictures, were thus reduced to sensational but momentary events. The problem of old-age homes—a subject of great personal interest to him—frightened the magazines; his pictures were "too disturbing, too revealing." Furthermore, the magazines often cropped his photographs ruthlessly, in order to force them into a given design format, or else reduced them in scale to a size incapable of evoking a powerful response in the viewer. A history of fifties magazine photojournalism would show the pictures the way they were used; my intention is rather to focus on the photography itself. The quotations that accompany the pictures, however,

An inadvertant self-portrait,
Park Forest, Illinois, 1953

are drawn from the publications themselves and accurately reflect the editorial inflection placed on the pictures in the magazines.

Most importantly, I find in Weiner's own writing a justification for a fresh wind, a wider view. He wrote: "I think that even working for the specific—being moved by that spirit of time and place—sometimes that exact instant may carry in it the seeds of a broader and more universal comment. Then even journalism need not always deal with the fleeting and transitory to be looked at for just a few moments and then forgotten." He was well aware that much of the work done in his own day by photographers "will not necessarily stand against a long, cool appraisal." Ultimately, he hoped that his own pictures would, and that they would become, in his words, "remembered images...images that will live and grow, and become more meaningful in a historical perspective." Judging from the photographs in this book, he passed his own test with flying colors.

Hess Brothers Caravan of Fashions touring rural
Pennsylvania, 1952

A Tribe's Tone and Texture

Lionel Tiger

As the fifties drew to a close I was in Ghana studying how independence affected its politics and administration. I lived on the University of Ghana campus in Legon, where one day an American came to teach business administration, innovative in those parts and for those times. He and his wife were agreeable people, and he must have been a good teacher. They celebrated their arrival with a party on the lush green lawn of their bungalow, which was framed by the classic fat bougainvillea blooms and other heavy-cream beauties of tropical vegetation. A long table covered with a white cloth was generously stacked with colorful foods. On the table also, direct from Michigan, was an electric punch bowl a yard high, symbol of an effervescent unity of modern technology and old-fashioned hospitality. It bubbled in relentless perfection, perhaps the first electric punch bowl ever seen in West Africa— an apt electrosilverplated memorandum about how America worked and played. It represented a special self-confidence during a period when *Fortune* magazine declared that "The Greater Export" of the U.S. was information about what made the economy tick.

How to characterize a decade? When a filmmaker sets an historical story the material facts of life can be depicted with accuracy and a sense of tone. A novelist can reveal the inner lives of people established in their setting, and can with certain details suggest the broader picture. Students of anthropology, conversely, are often told that one of the most significant aspects of a community is what it takes for granted. What did people take for granted in the fifties? Certainly it appears that people were content to enjoy a kind of restorative banality, protecting and enhancing their private domestic quiet after the phenomenal public horrors of the Second World War. And if we run our movie fast-forward to the sixties, we see that the fifties were also quiet by comparison with the next decade, when private convulsions surrounding self and sexuality and public traumas of a new war amid old politics erupted in unprecedentedly electric ways.

Human lives, however, don't stop because there is nothing larger-than-life for historians, movie moguls, or novelists to celebrate. Everybody must live twenty-four hours a day; with energy or reluctance, ambition or disillusion, efficacy or confusion, everybody must fill the hours between seven in the morning and eleven at night. They must also generate an image of what the day, week, month, decade, or life should be like and then live it. What activities and images dominated the fifties?

Court life at Park Forest, Illinois, 1953, from a contact strip.

I nominate driving, baby-sitting, home-building, and home improvement. A vast program of state and federal interstate road-building accelerated the development of communities based on the use of private cars rather than feet and public transport. Roads spread people out, luring them from the dense and intricate neighborhoods that cities are made of. They drove to shopping centers, which became the most influential socioarchitectural form of the twentieth century. The suburbs became populated and extensive, no longer subsidiary economic and social forces. People worked diligently to make things—and they shopped diligently to own them. In a quiet, deliberate pageant of interior gentrification, they feathered and Formica-ed their nests.

They needed those nests. Many lives were in formation. During the war, very few babies were born, for understandable reasons. (A country doctor in British Columbia told me that during the war he and his colleagues were allowed to use then-novel aspirator devices for relatively easy abortions. When the war was over and the correct husbands were back in the correct beds, the Royal Canadian Mounted Police came around to collect the instruments.) Between 1946 and 1948 a huge number of babies was born. In 1940 there were 2.6 million American babies

This year, it is estimated, American women will bear... 1,700,000 second children, a 91% increase over 1940.
—Fortune, *August 1953*

born. From 1946 to 1950, an average of 3.6 million were born each year, while the figures rose to 4 million in 1954. The all-time

high was 4.3 million in 1957—one new person every seven seconds.

These new families had to be housed, and housed they were—more bountifully than ever before. In 1950 the Department of Commerce estimated that in each of the following three years, 875,000 houses were going to be necessary. By and large they became available. Veterans Administration mortgages decisively boosted countless families into the home-owning class as down payments were reduced to "pebble size," in *Fortune*'s words, for houses economically practical on their own terms, supported by tax deductions, and linked to the workplaces by the government's new roads.

Nearly thirty million people were added to the American population. The first years of the fifties were defined by the care and housing and feeding of the very young and the very many. With families of up to five children common, a huge volume of goods had to be selected and used to support these families. It also took an enormous amount of work day in and night out to maintain what had become high standards of accommodation, health, and hygiene. What *McCall's Magazine* called "togetherness" in 1954 both described and encouraged the greater cooperation and increased time that parenthood demanded.

If families prospered, so, it appeared, did the nation. 1957 was another "Best Year Ever," while 1958 was marked by the third balanced Eisenhower budget in a row. Japan entered the United Nations for the first time in 1957; that same year there was talk of an American oil shortage. The USSR was still trying

38   37   38   39

to catch up with the West economically, hampered still by the intensity and extent of its military expenditure.

As the United States was economically stable, individual families could establish attractive financial goals and have some reasonable prospect of attaining them. However, the new goals were not only for material things. New notions of mental and psychological prosperity were emerging, too. Parents were hooked like shiny trout on a tantalizing dream of endless progress, which now included "personal growth." It was no longer enough to raise children to obey parents and other acceptable elders, to wash their hands, watch their manners, and prepare for lives of seemly reproduction and diligent productivity. Psychological standards could be set up and strived for. The special closed circle of the family was opened to admit the expert, who could bring into individual families the standards

Now, whether he knows it or not, every practicing public-relations man is an engineer too—a social engineer.... If the first half of the twentieth century was the era of the technical engineers, the second half may well be the era of the social engineers.
—Public Relations Journal,
quoted in William H. Whyte, Jr.,
The Organization Man, *1956*

and techniques that flowed from newly empowered social sciences. The skills of science were now applied to the dilemmas of everyday life. Private questions were addressed to the psychiatrist rather than the uncle, the social worker rather than the bowling partner. And the baby-sitter became a surrogate

a surrogate parent.

Experts affected the most basic relationships. Bizarre though it should have seemed to the supermammal of them all, bottle-feeding was defined as more advanced than the old way. Though the use of baby bottles had, of course, been voguish before the fifties, it became the menu of choice. Careful formulae determined how much formula each carefully calibrated babe should be offered (as if a breast-feeding mother could have any precise idea of her child's need). This was the manufacturers' dream because they could now sell to normal, healthy people a product to replace a normal, healthy process. Food and drug suppliers took the show on the road and fanned out across America and the world to convince new mothers of the modern virtues of the new high road of baby feeding.

The trend away from breast-feeding also became a metaphor for a forceful assault on private experience. Ozzie and Harriet were standard-bearers for the professionalization of intimacy, for its bureaucratization. Now private matters could be exposed to trained figures of authority. Introductory primers to psychobabble began to circulate throughout the land. There was reason to reject doing what had been done before, even if it had worked for one's forebears, because personal psychological fulfillment could take precedence over the moral and practical guidelines of tradition. The therapeutic quest was gaining ground. It became acceptable, even fashionable, to examine the inner psychological landscape.

Not without cause. Despite the reproductive enthusiasm of the community at large, individuals could only with difficulty acquire either information or opinion about the process that yielded babies—and all the secret opera that usually preceded it. In decent high schools boys were never officially told that girls menstruated, or why or how. When the girls were marched down to the gym for a "special class in hygiene" the lads upstairs knew that an inexplicable mystery was under review. Yet those who needed the instruction most received the least. They remained curious about a matter that thus became an Everest of allure and puzzled wonder. Matriculated males at distinguished universities across the country conducted often violent panty raids on females' dormitories. Though a fad and scandalous, such widespread public occurrences presumably revealed a facet of the private landscape of sexual bafflement.

But there was a broad embargo on visual and aural information about virtually anything between peoples' legs. Movies could not depict two unmarried humans in the same bed unless one acrobat maintained a foot on the floor. (Perhaps this accounted for the seemingly elongated stature of the great leading men.) But it didn't help youngsters hoping to square the formal lore of their culture with what they heard on the streets and experienced about their own bodies.

Once on a live broadcast—was it Milton Berle?—a particularly energetic dancer—could it have been Carmen Miranda?—danced with such extravagant aerobic enthusiasm that her halter top was dislodged for an instant. *Her real, factual breast was seen on national TV.* People talked about it for days. It is hardly surprising that Hugh Hefner's *Playboy* was almost instantly successful, despite its unprecedented violation of the existing boundary between pornography and journalism.

The relationship between public and private life remained uneasy, unexamined—the Kinsey reports on the male in 1948 and the female in 1953 appeared to astonish the citizenry. Suddenly sex seemed much more complicated than it was supposed to be. Family life had been held to be automatic, with narrowly appropriate ways of conduct. Nevertheless, Simone de Beauvoir's *The Second Sex* offered a major bulletin about the possible struggle to come. The book appeared in 1953, the same year as *Playboy* and the Kinsey report on females. Something was brewing, but one couldn't tell quite what, particularly from the well-tended homes and gardens of the busy, prolific families that had newly colonized the landscape. There seemed no reason to believe anything would disrupt their apparently nearly perfect lives.

If the international world of the fifties was confusing, it was not viscerally threatening. America had been the world's most thriving island culture, not isolationist but isolated: at the time,

Many of us know, or suspect, how heavily our postwar prosperity, above its cushion of defense spending, rests on the twin supports of new cars and new suburbs; in fact, the latter depends primarily on the former.
—*David Riesman,* Abundance for What? and Other Essays, *1964*

only about 4% of its trade was with the outside world. Like the Soviet Union, it had entered the Second World War a second-tier power, but with the destruction of everyone else's economic bases, America ended the war at the head of the line.

Next in line, however far down, stood the Soviet Union, with its decisively un-American ideology and its confused, belligerent self-justification. What to do about it? Joe Stalin, Joe McCarthy, Johnny Dulles, the China Lobby, Henry Luce, and others obliged with a massive, if imprecise, strategy of Cold War. A plausibly grand mythic enemy was created where no real one existed. Very few Americans had ever seen a real Russian. Furthermore, the last authentically bloody threat to Americans on American soil had been from other Americans. Eisenhower—a real soldier who had won a real war—was found to be the right non-politician to manage a non-war military buildup. Yet there was a real test in Korea. Inexplicably, it seemed to many, American men were sent to fight on Korean soil in a spasm that, somehow, barely disturbed the equilibrium of life at home. Perhaps it was a war too small and too far away to make much difference.

There was, however, always work and what it produced—things. A perfect consummation: people became successful by making things, and announced their success by owning and using them. Work was still redemptive. The rungs of the ladder had not yet acquired the aura of stations of the crass, as they would in the decade to follow. The phenomenal, invited intrusiveness of television offered a huge new opportunity for producers to advertise what they had crafted. Ad posters in shops boasted products AS ADVERTISED ON TV. Not only did advertisers find that they could reach more people more cheaply with television than with print, but people no longer turned to newspapers as before. Fewer and fewer newspapers struggled more and more.

Americans are exhibiting a furious interest in their homes. In part the interest has been enforced by the 33 million postwar babies (and by the cost of postwar baby-sitters). In part the interest is a product of TV. To some extent it proceeds from the lively sociability of the new suburbia.
—Fortune, *March 1954*

Everyone who could, viewed. A startlingly large, intimate web linked Americans to the new stars who represented the wider community to itself. "Good evening," said the newscaster familiarly, as if dropping in for a brew with forty million people.

Everywhere became a blue-light district.

The town meeting was reborn in reverse, a giant with a single, all-seeing eye.

The fifties faded to a paradox. On the one hand, there was the public reality of the cavalcade of new stars now shining in the home as well as in the neighborhood movie theaters. This firmament helped create an intensity of public symbolic life that would in the decade to come affect politics, business, and even warfare. On the other hand, there was also an articulated, inner landscape, full of urgency, grievance, needs, pride.

Individuals in a lonely crowd became aware that in their lives they would increasingly have to depend on their own resources, their own plans, their own skills as individual contractors to the society. Perhaps things were going well, but where were they headed? Things *looked* fine, but who could explain what was going wrong and what felt wrong? Things went one way, things went the other. What was going on?

One

Tastes and preferences have broadened and risen. Fenton Turck, consulting engineer, calls this elevation the "American Explosion," and compares it to the Periclean Age of Greece. He is jubilant about the increasing expenditures for books, photo developing and printing, higher education, flowers and seeds, phonographs and records, attendance at operas, the growing number of symphony orchestras and local opera companies. He also notes that design of draperies and furnishings is far better than before the war. He is, of course, right.

—Fortune, *August 1953*

When they test-drive the first atomic car, National Oil Seals will protect its bearings.

—*Advertisement in* Fortune, *1953*

PROSPECTS AND PROMISES

All history can show no more portentous economic phenomena than today's American market. It is colossal, soaking up half the world's steel and oil, and three-fourths of its cars and appliances. The whole world fears it and is baffled by it. . . . America's productivity is, of course, the world's highest.

—Fortune, *August 1953*

"Janet is studying marketing," one parent told me, "and she's only in the sixth grade. She's studying ads and discounts—things I didn't get until college. These kids are certainly getting a broad view of things."

—*William H. Whyte, Jr.,* The Organization Man, *1956*

C. Wayne Brownell, vice-president and industrial
relations director, Packard Motors, Detroit, 1952

Soldier on leave with friends, New York, c. 1950

Willard Garvey, head of Builders Inc.,
Wichita, Kansas, 1952

**The building boom is breaking all the
rules and records.**
—Fortune, *April 1952*

Welcoming the new baby, Park Forest, Illinois, 1953

In the Chicago area, a great many suburbs have either "Park" or "Forest" in their names, and two of them have both.
—*David Riesman,* Abundance for What? and Other Essays, *1964*

Section E-8 of the communal garden, Park Forest, Illinois, 1953

Researchers at the RCA–David Sarnoff Lab work on the
development of new TV recording apparatus, Princeton,
New Jersey, 1955

Exercise class, Park Forest, 1953

Social hour, organized by the Civic Association of Concord Park, an integrated housing development, Trevose, Pennsylvania, 1956

A study of Concord Park made by psychologist George Grier and his sociologist wife, Eunice, dramatically discloses that people are happier in mixed communities than segregated ones.
—*Newspaper clipping in Weiner's archive, source and date unknown*

Martin Luther King and family, Montgomery,
Alabama, 1956

Modern art exhibition at the Boston Arts Festival, 1956

The planning of Lincoln Center, New York City: (left to right) Wallace Harrison, Pietro Bellushi, Philip Johnson, and Gordon Bunshaft, undated

Stockholders arriving at General Motors annual meeting,
Wilmington, Delaware, 1955

*By car, bus, train, and plane the shareholders
arrived in Wilmington. Those coming by train were
met at the Pennsylvania and Baltimore and Ohio
Railroad Station by specially chartered buses—
GMC coaches, of course.*
—GM Annual Report, *1955*

General Motors Motorama, Atlantic City,
New Jersey, 1954

Campbell's Soup warehouse, Camden,
New Jersey, 1955

American Machine and Foundry, unidentified
location, 1955

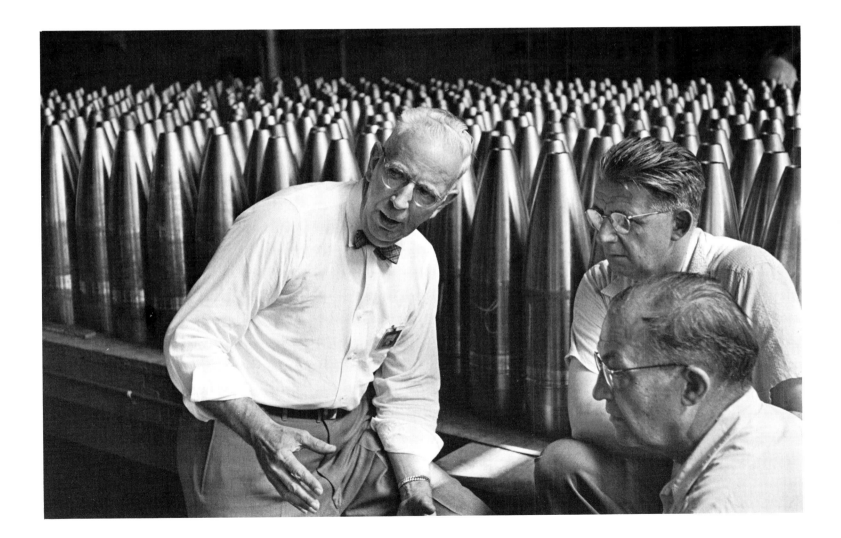

Plywood boxcar prepared for export to Saudi Arabia at the
Pressed Steel Car Company, Chicago, 1952

American trade exposition, Warsaw, Poland, 1958

Americans have re-outfitted, refurnished, and restyled their homes in a spirited revolution that has kept the furniture, appliance, and housewares industries in steady turmoil ever since the war.
—Fortune, *March 1954*

Businessmen assess an unidentified site for
development, c. 1951

Farm population has declined...centralized
population growth has stopped....In 1929 60% of
Americans lived in big cities or on farms; today
nearly 60% live in suburbs or small towns.
—Fortune, *August 1953*

Burlington Mills office workers checking inventory during
a corporate takeover, New York City, 1950

Leon Irwin, president of the Dock Board
of the Port of New Orleans, 1952

*Leon Irwin, an insurance man, serves on the board
without pay; in addition, he gave up hundreds of
thousands of dollars of port insurance business
when he took up the post, to comply with the law
that no commissioner can do private business
with the port.*
—Fortune, *June 1952*

Ralph Stolkin (left), operator in television, film, oil, and
cattle, with associates, Chicago, 1952

A maintenance inspector outfitted
in safety gear entering an empty
hydrofluoric acid storage tank at
a Pennsalt plant, Calvert City,
Kentucky, 1952

*Basic Agricultural Chemicals: Benzene
Hexachloride; Calcium Arsenate; DDT;
Endothal Defoliants; Sodium Arsenite;
Sodium Chlorate...*
—Pennsalt Company Annual Report, *1952*

One

Dr. J. Robert Oppenheimer at the
American Physical Society meeting,
Princeton, New Jersey, 1956

Two

ark Forest is not a venture in Utopia, but a shrewd business operation designed to meet some new social facts of life... The final plan was to build around a central shopping center. And houses on the periphery later. These would be merchandised at bargain rates. The real money would come from the waterworks and the company's cut (ranging up to 10%) of every dollar spent in the shopping market—a constantly rotating, nonsatiable market of 30,000 people, many of whom would ever be poised at that stage when families just begin to lay up possessions. In effect, a city was being built to provide a market.

—William H. Whyte, Jr., Fortune, *June 1953*

The up-and-coming thing, the trade press reports, will be a drive to put three cars in every garage.

—A consumer report, 1953

THE HARD SELL

Essentially Americans in the middle income group buy the same things—the same staples, the same appliances, the same cars, the same furniture, and much the same recreation.

—Fortune, *August 1953*

Suburbia is becoming the most important single market in the country. It is the suburbanite who starts the mass fashions—for children, hard-tops, culottes, dungarees, vodka martinis, outdoor barbecues, functional furniture, picture windows, and costume jewelry. All suburbs are not alike, but they are more alike than they are different.

—Fortune, *August 1953*

A Procter and Gamble salesman visits a food store in New York City, 1956

A perfume saleswoman with customers in a department
store, Washington, D.C., 1953

A fashion show on board
the New York, New Haven,
and Hartford Railroad's
Show Train, 1949

A ''Hostess Party'' given by a Stanley Home Products
saleswoman, Westfield, Massachusetts, 1954

*They use personally favored brushes to
demonstrate the selling technique that has
made Stanley rich.*
—Fortune, *February 1954*

Shoppers at a Brooklyn Department Store,
New York City, 1952

Shoppers at Macy's Department Store,
New York City, 1954

Family shopping for modern furniture, Brooklyn
department store, 1952

**Modern has become a good deal less extreme in
recent years, and is being increasingly blended
with traditional.**
—Fortune, *March 1954*

Shopper, New York City, 1952

Car salesman ''Smiling Jim Moran, The Courtesy Man,'' Chicago, 1952

Buick Glamorama, Atlantic City, New Jersey, 1954

Stockholders at General Motors annual meeting,
Wilmington, Delaware, 1954

*Two proposals of shareholders were voted down.
One requested the board of directors to find a
woman who could be nominated and elected to
the board.*
—GM Owners' Newsletter, 1954

Singer Rosemary Clooney performing at a telethon
to benefit the fight against cystic fibrosis,
New York City, 1952

President Patrick B. McGinnis of the New York, New Haven, and Hartford Railroad, at a speaking engagement, Bristol, Connecticut, 1955

Here McGinnis expresses horror over the way the road has been run.
—Fortune, *April 1955*

Senator Earl Clements campaigning in Kentucky, 1956

Prescott Bush campaigning for senator,
Connecticut, 1956

Minutewomen for Peace at the United Nations,
New York City, 1950

Best-selling author Dale Carnegie lecturing on "How to Stop Worrying and Start Living," unidentified location, 1951

The best formula I ever heard for stopping worrying goes like this:
1. Find out precisely what the problem is that is making you worry.
2. Find out the cause of the problem. I know there's nothing startling about this approach—but it works.
—*Advertisement, Massachusetts Mutual, January 1952*

We are now confronted with the problem of permitting the

average American to feel moral even when he is flirting, even

when he is spending, even when he is not saving, even when he

is taking two vacations a year and buying a second or third car.

One of the basic problems of this prosperity, then, is to give

people the sanction and justification to enjoy it and to

demonstrate [that] the hedonistic approach to his life is a moral,

not an immoral one. This permission given to the consumer to

enjoy his life freely, the demonstration that he is right in

surrounding himself with products that enrich his life and give

him pleasure must be one of the central themes of every

advertising display and sales promotion plan.

—Dr. Ernest Dichter, Motivations, April 1956

Three

One of the most costly blunders in the history of merchandising was the Chrysler Corporation's assumption that people buy automobiles on a rational basis.

—*Vance Packard,* The Hidden Persuaders, *1957*

THE HIDDEN PERSUADERS

You have to have a carton that attracts and hypnotizes the woman, like waving a flashlight in front of her eyes.

—*Gerald Stahl, Package Designers' Council, quoted in*
   The Hidden Persuaders, *1957*

The persuaders, by 1957, were also learning to improve their skill in conditioning the public to go on unrestrained buying splurges when such images as mother and father were held up. . . . Mother was still the best image in relationship to sales.

—The Hidden Persuaders, *1957*

Packaging discussion for Procter and Gamble's *Tide*
at Benton and Bowles advertising agency,
New York City, 1956

The TV commercial is Procter and Gamble's most important advertising weapon.
—Fortune, *March 1956*

The floor manager directing audience applause during a live broadcast of a *Tide* commercial, New York City, 1956

The floor manager directing audience applause during a
live broadcast of a *Tide* commercial, New York City, 1956

Rehearsal for a General Motors presentation, Atlantic
City, New Jersey, 1954

Advertising campaign for Dana perfume at the Ritz
Carlton Hotel, New York City, 1950

Stanley Home Products vice-president
Albert Francis Regensburger demonstrating
sales technique to company dealers,
Westfield, Massachusetts, 1954

*The dealer explains how the brushes
sing—"Listen to the music of the
bristles"—and stomps on them to
demonstrate their durability.*
—Fortune, *February 1954*

Stanley president Catherine Loretta
O'Brien demonstrating sales
techniques to company dealers,
Westfield, 1954

President James Nance (second from left) and other
Packard Motor Company executives discuss styling at
company headquarters, Detroit, 1952.

Burlington Mills' Herbert M. Kaiser,
head of the hosiery division,
discussing promotional strategies,
New York City, 1949

Professional coffee taster,
W. R. Grace and Company,
New York City, 1952

By the midfifties, the major producers
of instant coffee were energetically
building emotional overtones and
social status into their product,
—*Vance Packard,* The Hidden
Persuaders, *1957*

William B. Murphy, president of
Campbell's Soup Company, at a
top-level soup-tasting, Camden,
New Jersey, 1955

Packaging decisions by Benton and Bowles agency
executives for Procter and Gamble products,
New York City, 1956

**Procter and Gamble wages psychological warfare
on many fronts.**
—Fortune, *March 1956*

Children shopping in a supermarket, Park Forest, Illinois, 1953

Studio back lot, Hollywood, California, 1953

Studio back lot, Hollywood, 1953

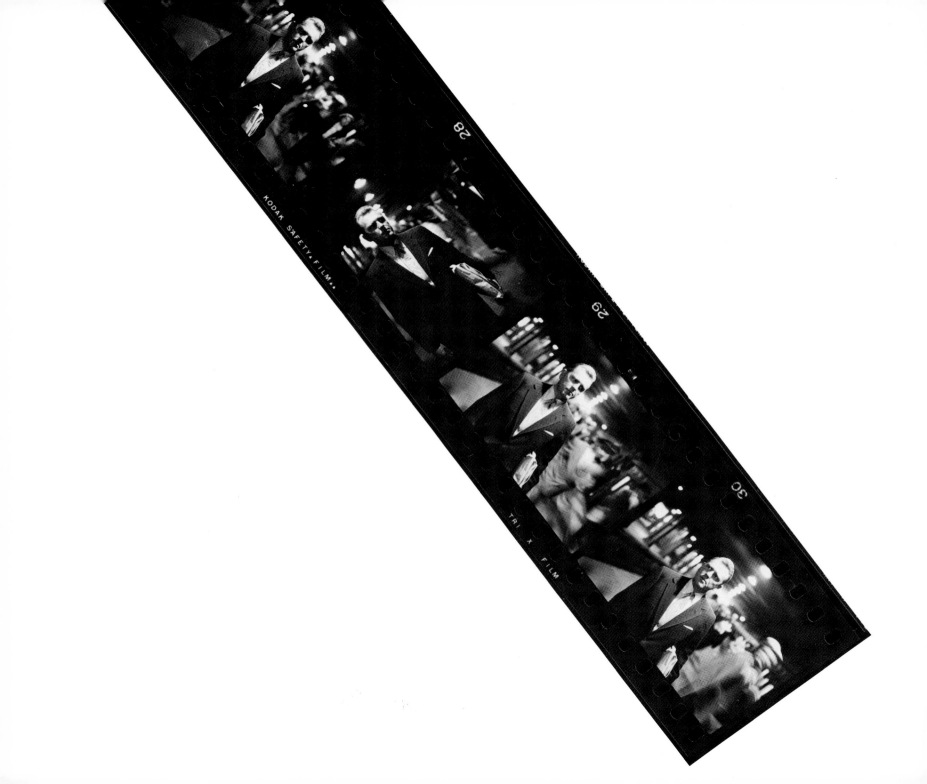

Four

*Y*OU CAN ALWAYS GET ANYBODY TO DO WHAT YOU WISH,"

the textbook proclaims. To this end the students spend four

months studying a battery of communication techniques and

psychological principles which General Electric tells them will

help them to be good managers. (Sample principle: "Never say

anything controversial.")... Though G.E. has no reason to

believe its trainees are ideologically unsound, it explains that

the course will help them "detect any bad guidance they receive

from union and political leaders, and even from educational

and spiritual leaders."

—*William H. Whyte, Jr.*, The Organization Man, *1956*

The younger men are sanguine. They are well aware that organization work demands a measure of conformity—as a matter of fact, half their energies are devoted to finding out the right pattern to conform to.

—*William H. Whyte, Jr.,* The Organization Man, *1956*

ORGANIZATION MAN

"The layout [of this house]," said the estate agent, "would not be acceptable to the corporation man. . . . It has the built-in bookcases. Those are the real drawback. Most of the young executives don't own books."

—*Vance Packard,* The Pyramid Climbers, *1964*

The head of a construction company feels that more important than belonging to the right club is [the] ability to behave in the knowing manner once inside. . . . At the table, he said, the well-schooled executive is likely to say to his guest, without looking at the menu, *"Wouldn't you like some oysters?"*

—The Pyramid Climbers, *1964*

Henry Kaiser and top management in telephone
conference, Oakland, California, 1951

Corporate recruitment at Michigan State University, East Lansing, 1957

Getting on friendly terms with faculty people is, of course, an important part of a recruiter's mission, and in this branch of their work Irwin and his colleagues get valuable guidance from a special "Engineering and Science College Directory" compiled by G.E. Among other things, the directory shows the size and nature of any grants made to a college from G.E. funds and lists the names of any faculty members who have ever been retained by G.E. as consultants, or who have been guests at G.E.-sponsored conferences or symposia.
—Fortune, *March 1957*

Potential trainee awaits interview at Michigan State
University, East Lansing, 1957

At General Electric's Edison Club, members check their
golf scores, Schenectady, New York, 1953

All trainees, employees with college degrees, and
men with supervisors' ratings are eligible to join.
For after-hours recreation . . . they can meet after
classes to play golf, bridge, and enjoy a planned
series of parties and dances.
—Fortune, *October 1953*

Four

Getting along with one's peers is important, in class and after-hours camaraderie. A trainee takes his schooling as a member of a group, not as a lone individual.
—Fortune, *October 1953*

A group of trainees tour G.E.'s turbine works, Schenectady, New York, 1953

Trainee Smiley accepts for the opportunities the position allows despite doubts about how the traveling will affect his wife and family.
—Fortune, *October 1953*

General Electric Division Manager G. I. Coons offering a position to trainee R. E. Smiley on G.E.'s traveling auditing staff, Schenectady, New York, 1953

Packard Motors President James Nance (third from left)
meets with executives, Detroit, 1952

The president has turned loose thunder and lightning at Packard.
—Fortune, *November 1952*

Robert Emmett Elliott, head of
New Orleans Petroleum Company
and head of International House,
a businessmen's association,
meeting with Boy Scouts,
New Orleans, 1952

Four

Edgar Kaiser, Eugene Trefethen, and Henry Kaiser in conference, Oakland, California, 1951

Sloan Fellows of the School of Industrial Management at
M.I.T. at their 1956 reunion, listening to Professor Erwin
Schell, who founded the program, Cambridge,
Massachusetts, 1956

*As at all reunions, the old grads tended to dwell on
the more intangible benefits of their Sloan year,
the good times, the "broadening influence"—and
they meant every bit of it. Just the same, amidst
the banter about putting on a little weight there,
eh, Charley, the alumni were extremely curious
about how the others had progressed—and not
just their inner growth either.*
—Fortune, *June 1956*

Wives of the Sloan Fellows socializing at the 1956 reunion, Cambridge

An office party at Stanley Home Products, Westfield,
Massachusetts, 1954

*The Management Man has become the real
migratory worker of the U.S.*
—Fortune, *May 1953*

Moving day, Park Forest, Illinois, 1953

Patrick B. McGinnis, president of the New York, New Haven, and Hartford Railroad, in his private coach with his chief engineer and others, 1955

Commuters arriving home on the
4:51 from Chicago, Park
Forest, Illinois, 1953

Five

From the time she places a cardboard crown on the hostess's

head to the time coffee is served, the accomplished dealer runs

her show with economy and flawless timing, pursuing steadily

her twin aims of selling merchandise and booking more parties.

She smiles, tells everyone how much "I am enjoying my work

and especially this party. Honest I am." She pointedly calls the

guests by their first names, or, collectively, girls. She jokes:

"This, girls, is a jewelry brush, for the rings in your bathtub."

She leads simpleminded games, like scattering beans on the

floor and handing out straws for the guests to draw them up.

The guest who captures the most beans gets a vial of perfume,

or perhaps salt and pepper shakers.

—Fortune, *February 1954*

The garden club now absorbs more of the wives' excess energies than any other activity.

—William H. Whyte, Jr., The Organization Man, 1956

A WOMAN'S WORLD

Even staying at home I do a lot more than you think. I act as Dick's secretary and handle all the phone calls when he's away, and then there's my League of Women Voters and the P.T.A. and the Great Books Course.

—Quoted in William H. Whyte, Jr., The Organization Man, 1956

Scientific planning applied to one housewife's method of making gingerbread reduced her travel in kitchen from 166 to 42 feet. Under old system, trips to and from center table and pantry added unnecessary footage. Now she centralizes movement by such improvements as utilizing built-in work areas and moving spices from pantry to cupboards.

—Collier's, November 1953

Executive assistant Helen Newlin at work on the golf
course, Los Angeles, California, 1955

Executive assistant at work in her boss' car,
Los Angeles, 1955

Secretary with boss, Henry J. Kaiser, Oakland, California, 1951

Easter bonnet display,
New Orleans, 1958

Women, returning to their suburban homes after a
matinee, glimpse a movie star at Grand Central Station,
New York City, 1953

Arthur Miller and fans after a reading at the 92nd Street
YMHA, New York City, 1956

Pool shark's girl friend,
New York City, 1955

Kaffeeklatsch, Park Forest, Illinois, 1953

Just as the Bunco player may put his mind to mastering bridge, so the Ph.D.'s wife learns to have fun at a coffee.
—Fortune, *July 1953*

Get-together, Park Forest, 1953

115

Nursing student, New York City, 1955

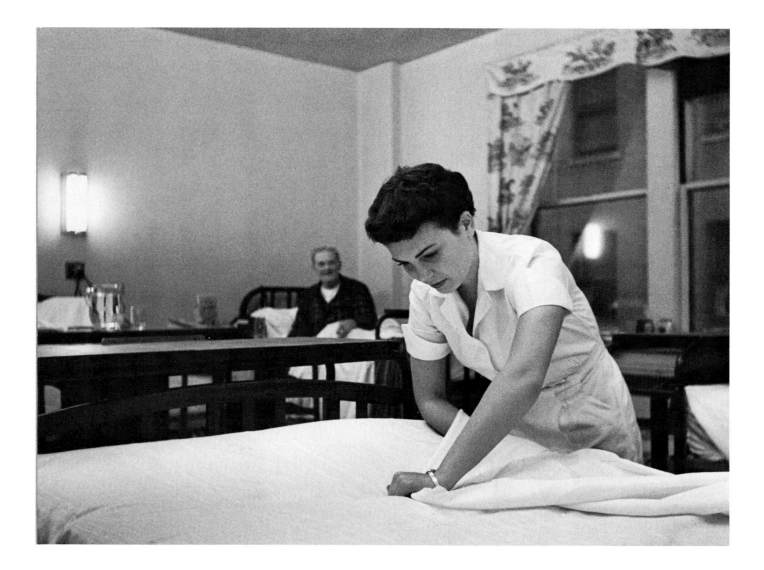

High-school teacher,
New York City, 1953

The young women from Mills stop the housewives in the street and ask questions. There are lots of questions. The answers portray family life in that particular community. The answers tell about the children who go to the school down the street. The questioning students from Mills had never known the makings of a community. Now they know.

—''Who Cares About Teachers?'' Mills School Report, *undated*

Student teachers on a field trip,
New York City, 1955

Models preparing for a fashion
show on board a commuter
train of the New York, New
Haven, and Hartford Railroad,
1949

Pedestrians on Fifty-seventh Street,
New York City, 1950

Pedestrians on Fifty-seventh
Street, New York City, 1950

*E*very minute [in Park Forest] from 7:00 A.M. to 10:00 P.M.

some organization is meeting somewhere. Looking through the

picture windows of one of the community buildings one typical

night I saw: on the top floor, the church choir rehearsing; the

Explorer Scouts (waiting for a quorum to plan next week's hike);

world politics discussion group (to discuss what causes war; a

second discussion group was to meet on a different evening to

discuss American foreign policy). Bottom floor: school board

meeting (to talk over interior decoration of the new school); an

organizing committee to organize a new organization (the

Protestant Men's Club); Husanwif Club (to watch slides on

safety rules for children).

—William H. Whyte, Jr., The Organization Man, 1956

Six

Appliances deliver a higher standard of living in a given number of woman-hours. And the work-saving appliances have also helped the housewife decide she has time for a huge family.

—Fortune, *March 1954*

NUCLEAR FAMILIES

"I sort of look forward to the day my kids are grown up," one sales manager said. "Then I won't have to have such a guilty conscience about neglecting them."

—*William H. Whyte, Jr.,* The Organization Man, *1956*

I'd like six kids. I don't know why I say that—it just seems like a minimum production goal.... Nothing is as human as a child.

—*Quoted in David Riesman,* Abundance for What? and Other Essays, *1964*

Save for a few odd parents, most are grateful that the schools work so hard to offset tendencies to introversion and other suburban abnormalities.

— The Organization Man, *1956*

"Father of the Year," unidentified location, 1952

James Conkling, president of C.B.S. Records, at home, with his family, in Bronxville, New York, 1955

James Conkling lives like a TV program, on a split-second schedule. While he brushes his teeth, his wife shows him a breakfast menu, which may include chocolate pudding. By nine o'clock he is on a train for Manhattan. Around 7:00 P.M. he gets back to Bronxville. After a brisk dinner (no cocktails), and sixty minutes of playing with the children, he plows into a mound of work.
—Fortune, *March 1957*

Morris L. Levinson, president
of Rival Dog Food, and family,
Scarsdale, New York, 1956

John S. Justin, Jr., president of
an old family firm, A. H. Justin
and Sons of Fort Worth, Texas,
which makes cowboy boots, 1956

Edwin and John Mosler with their
mother at their Manhattan home,
1956

Edwin takes the responsibilities
very seriously....John is a more
lighthearted type, and is rather proud
that his booklet, "What You Should
Know About Safes," became a very
popular item in prison.
—Fortune, *August 1956*

The Woodle family, Harrison,
New York, c. 1955

Six

A goodbye party for one of the gang.
—Fortune, *July 1953*

Party in the "tot yard," Park Forest, Illinois, 1953

Teenage party, Greenville, South Carolina, 1957

Early in the evening the girls' group sat on one side while the boys kept frozen, which continued until refreshments came and the party livened up. They played games and then had refreshments which the girls themselves had prepared.
—Colliers, *June, 1957*

Adult party, Park Forest, Illinois, 1953

The Fritz Thomas family, during a period of catastrophic
floods, Mondamin, Iowa, 1952

The Thomas family, Mondamin, 1952

An unidentified family living in poverty, Washington, D.C., 1952

Grandparents with child, Blue Rock,
Nova Scotia, 1950

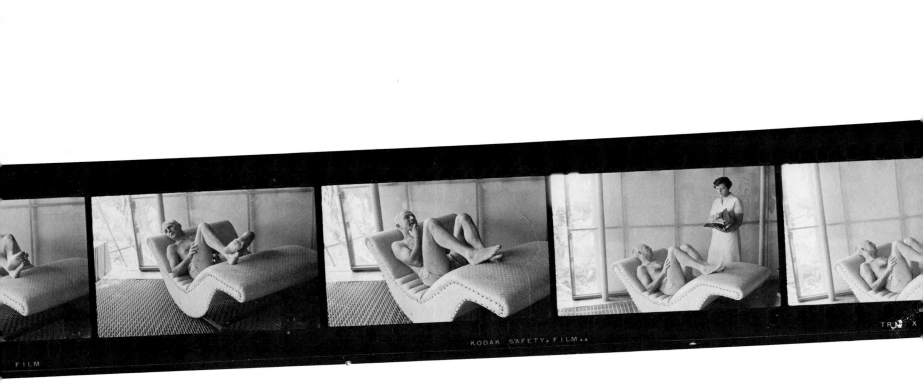

Seven

*A*t forty-four he has three main ambitions: to build, make friends, and enjoy himself. His firm grosses around $4 million a year, mostly on military housing projects. His friends include Hollywood stars, Texas oilmen. His $250,000 house, built into the side of a Hollywood hill, is not so fantastic as it looks, he says. He uses it as a testing laboratory for ideas for homes, e.g., a light fixture that shuts off at a sharply spoken "Off"; a bomb shelter with lead doors. Haye's shelter may be entered through a swimming pool; refugees from an A-bomb blast, he says, can wash off radioactive dirt before plunging into the tunnel.

—Fortune, *June 1955*

One ad agency executive explained with fervor: "What makes this country great is the creation of wants and desires."

—The Hidden Persuaders, *1957*

SUCCESS STORIES

Not all the young presidents, however, are self-made men, a fact they like to illustrate with a standard joke. "When I was out of the army," it usually runs, "I went to work for a small company. After a couple of years, the president called me in and said, 'I've got news for you; I've decided to make you the new president.' I said, 'Gee, thanks, Dad.' " This always gets a laugh.

—Fortune, *August 1956*

"Well, ladies and gentlemen," Garry said, "I'm through racing after your mechanical rabbit. I'm not going to climb any further up your blasted ladder. This is where I get off."

She got up somehow on wobbly knees and went to meet him between the tables. His strong arm held her close against his chest.

"To love and to cherish," he said softly.

"To love and to cherish," she repeated.

—*"Fireworks for Michelle,"* Ladies' Home Journal, *May 1953*

The New Rich: *Twin symbols of the prosperity of Texas's Ross Sams are the Cadillac and the trim Baptist Church.*
—Fortune, *January 1952*

Ross Sams, church furniture maker, Waco, Texas, 1955

Kenneth Spencer, head of Spencer Chemical Company,
Kansas, 1952

*Six-foot-two inches of spring steel... His
unconservative income in 1950: $500,000... runs
his company as much from the air as from the
ground.*
—Fortune, *January 1952*

William L. Graham, real-estate and oil operator, Wichita, Kansas, 1952

William Mullis, head of the Trade Winds Company,
pioneered the commercial marketing of frozen shrimp,
breaded and ready to fry, Savannah, Georgia, 1952

His 500 employees—none of whom are Chinese—work in two shifts and turn out over twenty-five different Chinese food products at the rate of 250,000 units a day.
—Fortune, *August 1956*

Jeno Paulucci of Minnesota heads the Chun King Company, a firm specializing in frozen Oriental foods, 1952

Joachim has made a fortune out of secondhand burlap bags, trading on high U.S. demand plus shortages created by postwar discord between jute-supplying Pakistan and jute-weaving India.
—Fortune, *January 1952*

Sam Joachim, head of Imperial Bag Company, Dallas, Texas, 1952

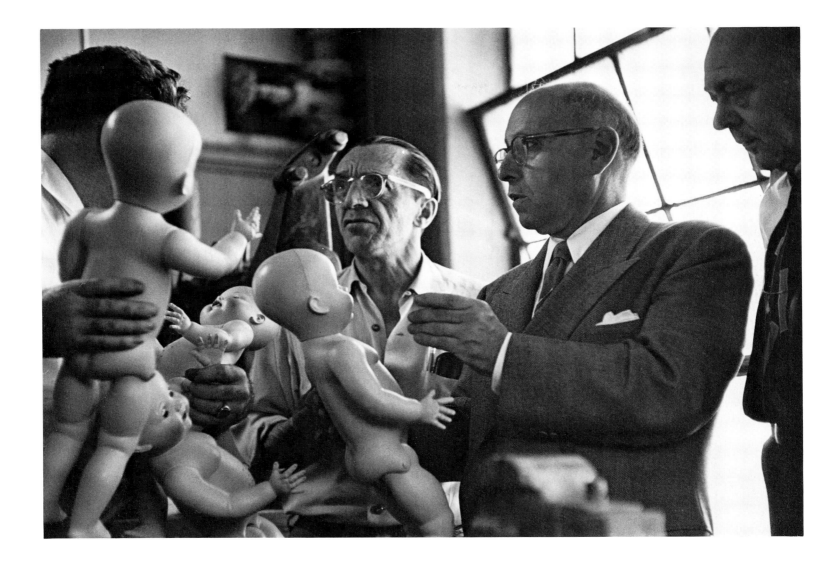

Abe Katz (second from right), head of Ideal Toy
Corporation, maker of Plastic Flesh dolls,
New York City, 1952

*Here he and some workmen hold a conference
over the right shade of blue for a doll's eyes.*
—Fortune, *January 1952*

The big wheeler-dealer from Texas...Texas couldn't hold Clint Murchison.
—Fortune, *January 1953*

Clint Murchison, oil operator from Texas, playing gin rummy aboard his DC-3, *The Flying Ginny*, with Wofford Cain (extreme left) and Sid "Big Rich" Richardson, 1953

John Olin, president of Olin Industries,
at Nilo Farm with King Buck,
Illinois, 1953

*Olin spends part of his free time
working to increase the game supply,
whose size is the main barrier to bigger
sales of arms and ammunition.*
—Fortune, *November 1957*

Hal Hayes, a builder, with his custom Cadillac, Bel Air,
California, 1955

Hayes holds a meeting in his home in Bel Air, 1955

A guest arrives at El Morocco, New York City, 1955

Harold Arlen (partly hidden), Marlene Dietrich and Truman
Capote at El Morocco, 1955.

The Duchess of Windsor and Charles Cushing at
El Morocco, 1955

Designer Oleg Cassini
with mambo dancer
Miss Rivera at
El Morocco, 1955

El Morocco, 1955

El Morocco, 1955

Actress Rhonda Fleming and Prince Christian of
Hannover at El Morocco, 1955

Milton Berle on stage
at El Morocco, 1955

Eight

The average shoplifter, the police chief told the newspapers, was not a low-income wife; she was the wife of a junior executive making $8,000, she belonged to a bridge club, was active in the P.T.A., and attended church. Usually she had about $50 a week to spend on food and sundries. Perplexed, the police chief and the village chaplain had to put it down as part of "the middle class neurosis." ... Perhaps ... they stole to be caught— as if they were asking to be punished for wearing a false face to the world.

—William H. Whyte, Jr., The Organization Man, 1956

A man who paints his garage fire-engine red in a block where the rest of the garages are white has literally and psychologically made himself a marked man.

—Fortune, *August 1953*

THE LONELY CROWD

The day the Johnsons moved away . . . they suddenly got cold feet and hated to leave town. In the new city they were going to so much would be strange. . . . But not everything will be strange. The grocer and the druggist will have unfamiliar faces, but the products they carry will be old friends. The shelves of every store will be stacked with brand names the Johnsons recognize.

—Advertisement for Brand Names Foundation, *Collier's, December 1950*

A depression? They don't even think about it. If they are pressed into giving an opinion on the matter, their explanations would suggest that America has at last found something very close to the secret of perpetual motion. And the gears, they believe, can no longer be reversed.

—William H. Whyte, *Jr.,* The Organization Man, *1956*

Bureaucrat, Washington,
D.C., 1953

Census taker, New York City, 1949

Subway riders at Herald Square,
New York City, 1951

New Year's Eve, Times Square, New York City, 1951

News vendor, New York City, c. 1953

Lack of such amenities, conversely, is also noted. In one suburb, to cite a rather extreme example, a couple were so sensitive about the bareness of their living room that they smeared their windows up with Bon Ami—and kept them that way until the new dinette set arrived.
—Fortune, *August 1957*

Shopper, Brooklyn, New York, 1952

Backstage at a circus, New York City, c. 1954

Crowd at the laying of the United Nations cornerstone,
New York City, 1949

The Third Avenue El,
New York City, 1951

Montgomery, Alabama, 1956

Bus boycott, Montgomery, Alabama, 1956

Soldier on leave,
New York City, 1950

*Civilian indifference, and even
hostility, greet servicemen on leave.*
—This Week Magazine, *April 1950*

Sailors on leave, New York City, 1950

Commissioners of an old-age home indicted on charges
that twenty-nine residents died of malnutrition, near Fort
Wayne, Indiana, 1951

Male residents of the old-age home near Fort Wayne,
Indiana, 1951

Police lineup, Detroit, 1951

Sex crime is a big part of it. The number of molestations, rapes, gang rapes, homosexual maraudings, abuses of children, and psychopathic episodes police carry as "indecent liberties" is to the outside observer shocking and ominous.
—Collier's, *November 1949*

Murder scene, Washington, D.C., 1951

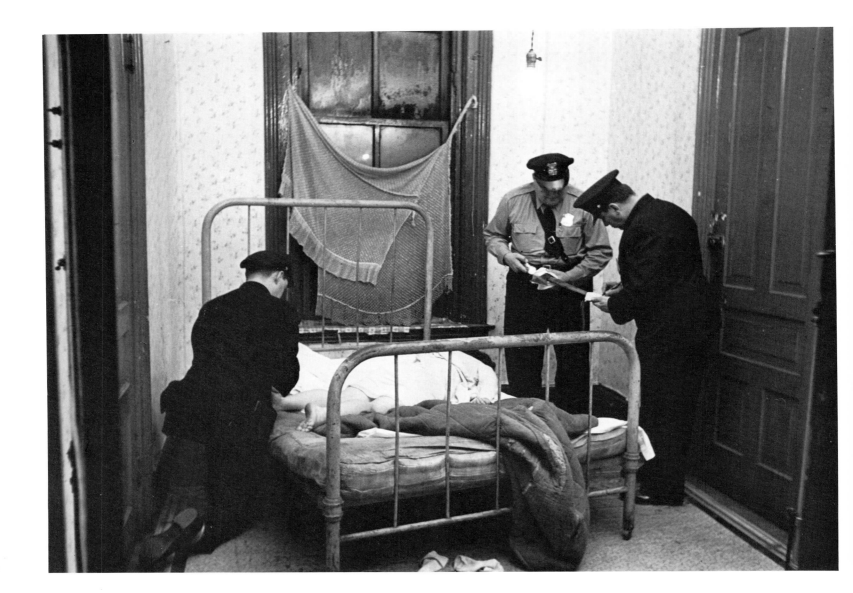

Sergeant Leo W. Gannon and Captain Pat J. O'Reilly,
acting inspectors of a division, checking on a police signal
box, Boston, 1951

Women returning home to their boardinghouse in
Philadelphia; the neighborhood was the scene of many
molestations and attacks, 1950

Psychiatric hospital on Long Island, New York, 1950

Atlantic City, New Jersey, 1955

How Weiner Worked

William A. Ewing

Dan Weiner was born in New York City on October 12, 1919, the son of Russian-Rumanian parents for whom America did not prove a golden land of opportunity. Dan's father was a poor breadwinner; in light of his own failure he was distressed when his son began early on to show a keen interest in painting. In spite of parental displeasure—ironic, since his father would eventually achieve some success as a naive painter—Dan continued to paint. The gift of a large-format Voigtlander camera from his uncle on the boy's fifteenth birthday triggered an interest in photography as well. After several years studying painting at the Art Students League and Pratt Institute, working by day to earn a living, Dan turned full-time to photography, soon landing a job with a commercial photographer.

Weiner found encouragement, a social conscience, and deep friendships as a member of the Photo League, an idealistic and energetic association of photographers that eventually fell prey to McCarthyism. In his Photo League years, Weiner was particularly close to the work of the great documentary photographers of the Depression: Dorothea Lange, Walker Evans, Russell Lee, and others who participated in the Farm Security Administration program. "Dustbowls, breadlines, and Hitlerism"[1] were images of lasting influence.

Drafted into the armed forces in 1942, Weiner served as a photography instructor in the Army Air Force until the end of the war. Although he hated army life—and the rural outpost in Georgia where he was stationed—it was in the army that he was introduced to the small, versatile 35mm camera. He took to the tiny Contax, in the words of his widow, Sandra, "as if he'd been using an eye-level camera all his life." By war's end he was poised for a career as a professional photojournalist—an auspicious moment, since the great picture magazines were approaching their zenith. "My generation is probably the first in history," Weiner wrote, "to become conscious of the great forces that are at work in our society through the visual media—the magazine, the newsreel, television—rather than the written word." Confidentially he predicted, "The most important photographs of the next half-century will be made in photojournalism."[2]

He believed he was about to join the noble ranks of the American documentarians. He decried limpid self-expression in photography, with its often facile romanticism. "Photography is too often used for its decorative and entertainment qualities," he argued. "We must resurrect this word 'documentary.' " But documentary, he added, "does not necessarily mean turning the camera only on the disinherited." The photographer should shape and color significant events. Weiner was fond of quoting the writer Joyce Cary on the work of Trollope. The novelist, Cary maintained, found in life what we all find, "a mass of detail without meaning," but responded by forging an art that said, "This is the shape of things to come under the confusion of appearances. These are the forces which really move people to action."[3] These observations crystallized Weiner's own convictions.

Not content to document passively what went on around him, Dan Weiner understood the art of intelligent filtering. He yearned to express through photography—more precisely through the vehicle of photojournalism—his *faith*: faith in humanity, in society, and in photography itself as a means of communicating and celebrating fundamental values. "Now comes the challenge," he wrote, "of making photography as flexible as life itself. To probe and parry and explore the deeper recesses of society's mores."

In a speech to fellow photographers on the picture story, Weiner decried the unimaginative beginning, middle, and end format of storytelling employed by most of the illustrated magazines. "How many picture stories have we seen" he reminded his audience, "with 'Day in the Life' of a Young Actress, Ballet Girl, etc.? She gets up in the morning—ah, chance for a leg shot! Breakfast at the drugstore—she's poor!—and so on.... All too often the picture story gets to look like a comic strip." Instead, Weiner argued, the photojournalist should work with the looser essay concept, which develops nonlinearly, organically, without a preconceived structure. He also stressed the importance of sensitizing oneself to the subject matter before taking the actual pictures—studying the subject, without anticipating what the pictures will *look* like. So informed, one's understanding becomes more acute, one's discrimination is sharpened.

Seeing his own images in print was another matter. Weiner never assumed that his intentions would be honored by editors and art directors. Thoughtless cropping, reducing the pictures' sizes and thereby diminishing their effectiveness, paring a fully developed story down to skin and bones, these were the rule rather than the exception. Of his story on the Montgomery bus boycott in *Collier's* Dan complained: "The Montgomery pictures were used to illustrate something quite out of context. My point was to show the great forces struggling here in one area. And I felt it had great historical importance. What happened was that the pictures were used out of context, and the whole idea was dissipated."[4] And lest it appear that he was singling out *Collier's*, he added, "The attitude at *Collier's* was no different from many other publications that use photographs." Weiner never reconciled himself to the "pat and slick formulas of the magazines" and the "direction and domination of editors."

When compared with the original Weiner photograph on page 175, a reproduction from *This Week* magazine demonstrates the liberties taken by editors: the veil has vanished; all eyes have been dramatically retouched; eye contact between one of the women and one of the sailors has been definitively established (a contact by no means as certain in the original!). Further, the hairdos have been restyled, and two of the faces (the man at center and the woman at right) have been beautified according to conventional media standards.

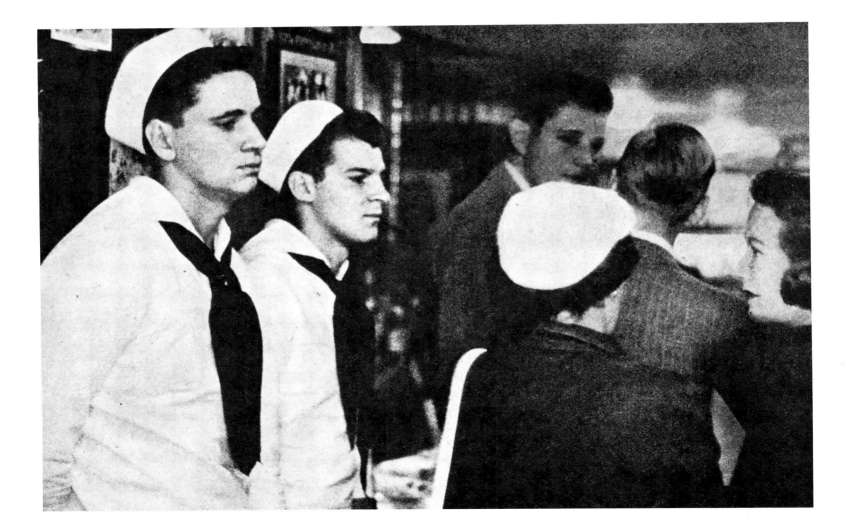

Sometimes, in fact, the tone of his work belied the editorial intentions of the magazine. When *Fortune* ran a story on Packard Motors ("Packard's Road Back," November 1952), it couched the story in heroic, frontieresque terms. The president of the corporation was described as "an exchampion...tooling along the comeback trail." The company was "reconquering the quality control market." And the president had "turned loose thunder and lightning" to accomplish his ends. But Weiner saw—and conveyed—a group of weary businessmen looking as if their problems were an insoluble mystery—and a monumental headache. Faced with this disparity between image and text, the caption writer described the scene as "the momentary calm found at the heart of a hurricane." It was a valiant attempt, but Weiner's gently mocking wit prevailed.

Weiner was ambivalent about the magazines. He believed the real value of his work lay in its being seen by large numbers of people. He couldn't accept the alternative routes of teaching or "art photography." Such photographers, he felt, ran the risk of navel-gazing, "turning introspective, precious."[5] "Photographers cannot produce in a vacuum," he explained. "They are very social beings. The worst aspect is being cut off from the magazines." But while he had to accept the magazines as the lesser evil, ultimately Weiner aimed for another kind of forum, possibly books. Seeking sponsorship from a foundation, he explained, "I'm interested in exploring the world and how people live and finding out how they are adjusting to the whole matter of industrialization and urbanization." In the meantime, "it took great belief, dedication, and necessity to continuously

thread one's way through all the pitfalls in a society that is against the reliable and the steady." The distinguished photographer Walker Evans, Weiner's colleague at *Fortune*, was to eulogize this "solidity of heart."[6]

The photographer drew in close to his subjects, physically and emotionally. However briefly, he enveloped himself in their lives: "The feeling of identification with the subject may give birth to some spontaneous and original ideas." Weiner knew that turbulent currents often lay beneath the smooth surfaces of social life. Up close, he was able to capture slight, unconscious, but telling gestures—a stolen glance, a fist clenched with anxiety. The critic Ben Lifson noted how the photographer was most acute when nothing much seemed to be happening. Then, "the smaller the gesture and the subtler the emotion, the more Weiner was engaged." (Note, for example, pages 36 and 163.) Lifson adds, "It is not absurd, in fact, to speak of his powers of observation in terms of Daumier's."[7,8]

Yet even up close, immersed in other people's intimacy, Weiner could move about as if cloaked in invisibility. When Weiner is at work, there is no intrusion: no one in the picture looks back at the photographer. People remain totally absorbed in their own world. William H. Whyte, Jr., the renowned sociologist with whom Weiner worked on several occasions, recalls how first he would work a room of businessmen in the manner of a local politician, cracking jokes, mingling, and generally putting everyone at ease.[9] He would then fade uncannily into the background; by the time he began to shoot, his presence was accepted with neither reserve nor confrontation. His was a cultivated strategy. Weiner did not, like an anthropologist, live with his subjects; his familiarity with them was a matter at best of days, and far more likely of hours, if not minutes. It was also a question of technique, of fluid camera movements that would not catch the eye of any participant. In this regard, Weiner was impressed by Henri Cartier-Bresson's dictum that the camera is an extension of the eye. "This is the most beautiful expression that I can think of," he told his wife, Sandra, "that photography has become as instantaneous as seeing." (Note, for example, how quickly he grasps the relationship between the anxious young man and the poster ideal of a recruit on page 91—or between the woman shopper and Gillette's ideal on page 58.)

Although he delighted in complex social interaction, he did not require exotic subject matter. Where other photographers might have despaired at the gray-suited uniformity of "organization man," Weiner reveled in the possibilities: "A board meeting suddenly becomes a tense drama, acted out around a mahogany table. Here is greed, aggressiveness, tensions detailed and characterized." Upon returning from an assignment on a particularly rapacious character, Weiner confided to a colleague, "I killed him that time!"

His compassion was reserved for ordinary folk, although his frames could still encompass high drama (page 57). Too, he was often able to portray a complex idea. What, for example, does a corporate takeover *look* like? Weiner illustrates one vividly (page 43). A study of "operators" (page 45), to use *Fortune*'s term, says much about the unsavory nature of their business that could not

be put into words, while his portrayal of uniformly attired businessmen restlessly prowling the land in search of development opportunities (page 42) speaks eloquently of their alienation from nature.

Composed, as he put it, to the edges of the frame, Weiner's pictures are busy, but they are never—contrary perhaps to first appearances—unstructured. He was acutely aware of everything going on in the camera field. As a result, the interest does not diminish as the eye moves from the center. (Note, for example, pages 65 and 133.)

Weiner typically shot hundreds of pictures for a story, and printed many more than the magazines could ever use; we have, as a result, an extraordinary archive of untapped material on the fifties. Although on occasion he used color, most of the material is in black-and-white. "I prefer my pictures colored by the imagination," he maintained, "rather than by Kodak."

Not all his work was shot on assignment. Many pictures were for his personal pleasure, or else, moved by a human plight, he undertook extensive projects, hoping to interest a magazine. One such story was on old age; another was on the Thomases, a farming family in Mondamin, Iowa, an area that was being ravaged by floods (pages 134 and 135). While his sincere concern earned him the Thomas family's profound respect, his work also brought home to them the magnitude and context of their own experience. Not long afterward he received this letter:

*We surely did enjoy the evenings we spend with you
and hope we can again see. My sister in law was sick*

*about not being able to say goodbye to you in person
and she says she enjoyed your visit a lot and she hoped
you felt welcome.*

*We got your pictures and we're going to make a
book of them for the Community Club. One never
knows though how forsaken and forlorn you look I
guess. I was practically ashamed of Peggy and I. We
really look horrid. I guess you can't be any better
looking than you are though.*

*I was so glad to get them and also to hear from you.
Different people had told me I'd never hear from you or
get any pictures either so I was very proud. They still
hadn't convinced me you were that kind of city fellow.*

*—Mrs. Fritz Thomas
Mondamin, Iowa, 1953*

**In these pictures, Weiner imparted a measure of the truly
heroic, even, perhaps, the saintly. Significantly, it was neither the
politicians, the business leaders, nor the entrepreneurs who
earned his greatest respect. "I carry with me always that great
body of photographs produced in the Depression of the thirties,"
he admitted. Although he would have been the last to make the
claim, the best of his work, such as the Mondamin flood story,
rivals that of his mentors.**

1. Weiner's words are taken from his diary entries and notes, which are in the hands of his widow, Sandra Weiner.

2. More of the photographer's thoughts may be found in "The Camera to Me," in *Dan Weiner 1919–1959*, ICP Library of Photographers, New York: Grossman Publishers, 1974, pp. 6–7. A collection of photographs is also included.

3. Joyce Cary, "On the Function of the Novelist," *New York Times Book Review*, October 30, 1949.

4. Weiner wrote: "I felt this was an historic occasion which I must try to record with my camera. I felt there was a new black in the South who was developing a new strategy of resistance to segregation with economic, legal and spiritual weapons. I thought too a longer-range "think" piece should be done in photographs of the less sensational but wider implications of this social phenomena. But I was not successful in convincing *Collier's* for whom I did these photographs in doing a large photo essay. A few of my photographs were used, along with some others to illustrate an article about the dilemma of the moderate in the South. Photography could have illuminated here a complex and historic situation. While I was in Montgomery I thought of something Alan Paton had said to me in 1954 when we traveled together on a story on the Negro in America. He said that "these people through their struggles to achieve their basic rights as citizens are reeducating us as to the meaning of true Americanism.""

5. In a review of an exhibition at the Museum of Modern Art, "Diogenes with a Camera II," he wrote: "On another wall the human photographs of Dorothea Lange face the ultimate in Siskind's effacement of traces of humanity...."

6. Evans was certainly in a position to know; if Weiner could be said to have had a mentor, it was this outstanding photographer Walker Evans, who had preceded him at the publication by five years.

7. Ben Lifson, in a *Village Voice* review of an exhibition at the Prakapas Gallery, New York, October 1980.

8. Most of Weiner's photographs were made with a 50mm lens, only occasionally supplemented by a 35mm wide angle.

9. Conversation with the author.

Often while on assignment Weiner found time for his
own decisive moments. New Orleans, 1958.

Index

Photographs from a number of Dan Weiner's original assignments have been separated in this book. The reader may wish to reconstitute the material as follows: Burlington Mills, pages 43 and 79; Campbell's Soup, pages 38 and 81; General Motors, pages 36, 37, 60, 61, and 74; Henry Kaiser, pages 89, 97, and 109; executives at work and home, pages 22, 86, 107, 108, 122, 126, 138, 139, 150,151, and 160; Montgomery, pages 33, 172, and 173; New Orleans, pages 44 and 96; the new rich, pages 45, 59, and 141 through 147; Packard Motors, pages 25, 78, and 95; Park Forest, pages 15, 18, 19, 28, 29, 31, 83, 101, 103, 114, 115, 131, 133, and 184; Procter and Gamble, pages 51, 68, 71, 72, 73, and 82; retail sales, pages 48, 52, 55, 56, 57, 58, 104, 105, 165, and 168; Show Train, pages 53 and 119; Stanley Home Products, pages 54, 76, 77, and 100; Patrick B. McGinnis, pages 63 and 102; presidents, pages 127, 128, and 129.

The contact strips are taken from Weiner's files on the following assignments: pages 2 and 3, General Motors; pages 6 and 7, Sandra Weiner (personal work)*; pages 22 and 23, executives at work and home; pages 48 and 49, retail sales; page 68, Procter and Gamble; pages 86 and 87, executives at work and home; pages 104 and 105, retail sales; pages 122 and 123, executives at work and home; pages 138 and 139, executives at work and at home; pages 160 and 161, executives at work and at home; and pages 184 and 185, Park Forest.

The photographs on the following pages were Weiner's personal work: 26, 84, 85, 110, 111, 112, 120, 121, 134, 135, 137, 166, 167, 170, 171, 183, and 191

*With apologies to Dan Weiner, the contact strip of his wife Sandra has been fabricated for design purposes from an original photograph.